WATERFALLS

BILLIE JEAN MANN

Waterfalls
Copyright © 2024 by Billie Jean Mann.

All rights reserved. No part of this book may be reproduced in any form or by any electronic or mechanical means, including information storage and retrieval systems, without permission in writing from the publisher, except by reviewers, who may quote brief passages in a review.

This publication contains the opinions and ideas of its author. It is intended to provide helpful and informative material on the subjects addressed in the publication. The author and publisher specifically disclaim all responsibility for any liability, loss, or risk, personal or otherwise, which is incurred as a consequence, directly or indirectly, of the use and application of any of the contents of this book.

MILTON & HUGO L.L.C.
4407 Park Ave., Suite 5
Union City, NJ 07087, USA

Website: *www.miltonandhugo.com*
Hotline: *1- 888-778-0033*
Email: *info@miltonandhugo.com*

Ordering Information:
Quantity sales. Special discounts are available on quantity purchases by corporations, associations, and others. For details, contact the publisher at the address above.

Library of Congress Control Number:	2024913717
ISBN-13: 979-8-89285-147-3	[Paperback Edition]
979-8-89285-146-6	[Digital Edition]

Rev. date: 08/28/2024

Contents

Acknowledgments	ix
Introduction	xi
Waterfalls—Broken Chain	**1**
This Too I Shall Overcome	4
Waterfalls— The Brighter Side	**7**
Finding Closure	11
I Never Stop Loving You	12
Ask God to Send You a Man	13
God's Chosen Rib	14
I Have Waited and Waited for Someone	15
What Matters the Most	16
Back in Love Again!	17
At Last! At Last! At Last!	18
Waterfalls—The Obstacle Side	**19**
When Your Life Flashes Before Your Eyes	23
Multiple Sclerosis (MS)	24
This Storm I Must Weather	25
Fight To Live Another Day	27
Waterfalls— The Peaceful Side	**28**
Death	32
My Life Here on Earth is No More	34
Heaven Awaits For An Angel Like Me	35
I'm Forever In Your Heart	36
A Mother's Dedication To Her Children	37
My Time Has Come To Say Goodbye	38
This Road I Will Travel No More	39
Time Ran Out For Me	40
I'll See You Come through the Pearly Gates Too	41
Waterfalls— Black Lives Matter	**42**
I Can't Breathe	45
Closing Remarks	**47**

Acknowledgments

"TO RISE FROM ANY FALL, I MUST STAND"

As my journey continues, this is how I stand. Every day of my life, I must acknowledge the Almighty God. God is my creator and knows all about me. He knows the good, the bad, and the ugly. He knows all of my faults and is aware of my failures. He knows what direction my life is going to go and will never leave me when trouble enters my path. This gift to write was given to me by God. It is truly a blessing.

To my daughter, Lydia, your ears are always available when I need someone to listen. I welcome your feedback and I know that any criticism is constructive and out of love. Thank you for being such a wonderful daughter and a great inspiration. Our bond is strong because we have had to endure so much and we have done it together.

I thank those individuals who have departed my life because their season with me ended. Thanks for understanding that in order for me to move beyond the dark areas of my life, I had to take my life in a new direction. Thank you for your support during our season together and I pray the support will continue as we maintain our friendship.

Time has its way of opening doors to allow others to be a witness and experience your journey up close and personal. I firmly believe that every door that opens-opens for a season and every door that closes-closes for a reason. This journey has not been easy nor has the path been full of light but thanks to my special friend who has been supportive and has been the light that shined on my path to help guide me through this journey.

To all my family, friends and readers, your support has motivated and encouraged me to continue on this journey. Thanks to my church family at Ebenezer United Methodist Church, Reidsville, GA. May your support and prayers continue.

Writing helps me fulfill my purpose in life. I am destined to be a motivator and an inspiration to others. I want to be a blessing in the life of others and I hope that by telling my story will allow someone, who is dealing with similar situations, "Overcome."

God Bless You All

Introduction

I was born and raised in Lyons, Georgia. I graduated from Lyons Senior High School. I was a straight "A" student voted "Most Intellectual" and "Most Likely to Succeed." Being voted "Most Intellectual" meant my peers considered me somewhat smart. I never had the nerves to leave Lyons, Georgia so I do not know how smart that was. I was always bound by relationships so I guess you can say I had book smarts but no common sense. Being voted "Most Likely to Succeed" has been somewhat of a challenge but I am a published author. I have also succeeded at being a mother. My daughter encourages me and lifts me up whenever I am at my weakest point. She has a loving and caring spirit and a heart of gold. My goal has always been to give her a true mother-daughter relationship that allows her the comfort to communicate with me about anything no matter how difficult the conversation maybe. I want her to feel free to express who she is and never belittle or think negative of herself because sadly enough, that's something society will have no problem doing.

As for me, I express myself through poetry. Writing is my therapy and a way to release pain and hurt that may cause me to walk around in bondage. The emotions and feelings I carry bundled inside are so much easier to say on paper. I have never been one to talk much but when I get in character, I become a different person. I love that emotional thrill I get when I am reciting one of my poems. Instead of seeking counseling, I just write. It allows me to release any anger that I maybe holding onto that would cause me to be bitter. Writing helped me learn to accept disappointment from others and let go so I would not keep disappointing myself. I learned to forgive which brought some much-needed closure. With closure, I was able to move on.

I grew up in the countryside of town and it reminds me so much of myself, very quiet. There is not much noise or traffic just wild animals and rugged dirt roads. What I like most about it is the peacefulness. It allows me to think without all the distractions. I hope one day to become a bestselling author, adding that to the list of accomplishments under my title earned, "Most Likely to Succeed."

"Waterfalls" is a book of poems where each one carries a message and holds their own reputation flowing rapidly like the water flowing down a waterfall, forming unique emotions. I love waterfalls because when I meditate to the sound of the steady movement of rushing water, it brings everything into perspective. The water does not flow backwards so I began to compare my life to the water in a waterfall. I realized that I was continuing to go backwards. I could not flow in life because like a tabletop waterfall not flowing that operates by batteries, my switch was turned "OFF."

Waterfalls
Broken Chain

Do not let a tragedy hold you in bondage. Break the chain and find a way to escape. Forgiveness is the key. Freedom comes when you use the key to unlock shackles from around life that is just weighing you down.

Forgiveness=Freedom

Waterfalls
Broken Chain

Why "Waterfalls" you might ask? I chose the title "Waterfalls" because I compared my life to the different stages that I witness in a waterfall. In the first stage, the water is barely moving. It is almost like a slow flowing stream of water where any particles or debris suddenly get stop by a rock or stump along its path. It takes a strong wind to shift the particles or debris back out into the path the water is flowing. In life, we can become stuck behind a rock or stump that will not let us flow, not even as a steady stream.

For years, I had been slowly flowing through life. I felt like a hostage in my own home. I kept myself isolated from society and whenever I went out, I was constantly looking over my shoulders. I had a wound that would not heal. When I wrote my first book, "The Best of Me Poetically," I removed the bandages off this wound. A tragedy that took away years of happiness from my life also stole my joy as well as my pride. I was unable to forgive this person for destroying me. I could say every year got easier to deal with but still I could not watch certain movies and a certain month of the year was always more difficult to get through.

I struggled with PTSD (Post Traumatic Stress Disorder). I was unable to sleep at night. I had to go through life like the particles flowing in a stream, always being stopped by the heaviness of this rock that constantly had me looking over my shoulders. Like a rock or stump, a chain is something that will hold you down. It will hold you back and not allow you to go but so far. I had to examine my life to see what chain was holding me back. I had some form of debris in my life that was stuck behind a rock, a stump, or held down by a chain. The sexual assault was a tragedy that left me with thoughts that I wanted my life to end. The outcome of my inability to forgive this person who had sexually assaulted me, literally made those thoughts come alive. I stopped living!

I suffered with anxiety and having panic attacks. I was functioning with the aid of medication just to find a way to cope. My family and friends saw how distant I was. There were mood swings, highs, and lows. There were times when I just wanted to disappear. I was almost to the point of having a nervous breakdown. It felt like I was wearing a vest full of dynamites tied around my chest. As I began to reflect back on the water as it flows in a waterfall, I did not see consistency. I did not feel the wind I needed to move this debris on downstream so my life could flow. What I needed was the power of God to break the chain in order for my life to start back moving.

I was going through some old papers to burn when I came across a poem I wrote over thirty years ago. I was dealing with the tragedy that happened to me when I wrote this poem and I thought the poem was lost forever. I remembered writing this poem and the more I wrote, the stronger I got. I went from being chained down-to feeling free. What a relief! I could now start to heal. I kept saying, "This Too I Shall Overcome," and from that this poem was birthed.

This Too I Shall Overcome

You were like a hound dog
That sniffed out my weakness
And took advantage of me

And then like a pit bull
You tore at my flesh
Until blood there was to see

As if it wasn't enough
To take away my pride
But my life you wanted too

I dare you to even think
That you should have took my life
When God gave me this life not you

What you took from me
Caused me to stumble
But God didn't let me fall

What you meant for bad
God turned around for the good
Now it's your face against the wall

How does it feel to cry out
And wish for your life to end
Cause no one comes to your rescue

Some people learn the hard way
You shouldn't do unto others
What you wouldn't want done unto you

The scars are there to remind me
Of the many hours I suffered
And the internal pain that left me numb

They are also there to remind me
That through Christ who strengthens
"This Too I Shall Overcome"

Repeatedly, I would read this poem not only to grasp hold of what happened to me but also to come to terms with it and be thankful that I survived such a horrific ordeal. I guess it is true what they say, "What doesn't kill you, makes you stronger."

Holding on to those painful memories was as if I had fallen and I could not get up. The things in life that causes us to stumble and fall can seem like you are emerged under water with weights tied around your ankles. Unable to hold my breath and unable to swim, I have no choice but to depend on God. I have to acknowledge God in all aspects of my life. Even in my time of trouble, in that darkest moment when I thought I would not make it back home, I was able to witness the power of God. Where I was begging for this monster, as I saw him, to kill me, God began speaking to me to show this person that I have a heart. It was something that I could not understand but I began to be sympathetic to someone who was clearly dying for attention. For just a few moments, my heart cried for the little boy trapped inside of this monster and to this day, I do not know exactly what I said to convince this person to let me go, but I know it was not me speaking. The slow stream of water flowing in a waterfall minus particles and debris, reminds me that as long as I have God's power flowing in my life, no harm done to me can keep me chained down.

Waterfalls
The Brighter Side

Happiness means you have crossed the bridge to Acceptance. Acceptance means no looking back.

Acceptance=Happiness

Waterfalls
The Brighter Side

There is a bright side to a waterfall. In stage two of a waterfall, the water is flowing rapidly. You see the consistency in the flow and an increase of speed as the water gets closer to the drop. Although, it is soothing in this stage, seeing the rush of water as it speeds up just intensifies the suspense of the unknown. I love the way a waterfall looks and sounds. A waterfall turned on in a room calms the atmosphere. My soul seems to be at peace when I sit and listen to a waterfall. The soothing sound of water flowing helps me meditate on my purpose in life and that is to inspire others. Being an inspiration to someone not only brings me a sense of joy but it helps to know that someone just needed to know how to make it through.

When I share my story, it is through poetry. It allows me to open up about the experiences I have had to get through. Through poetry, I can release those emotions that have been hidden away causing a buildup of bitterness, anger, and hardening of the heart. There maybe someone I encounter that is hurting and cannot let go. I have learned that holding on to someone is exhausting. When you cannot let go of someone who does not love or feel the same way you do, you are just aging. I learned to love me and put a value on my time. Time is something you cannot get back. When you allow someone to put your heart in a box, it only keeps the dust off it. Just like a piece of fruit sitting idle on the table, it eventually gets hard and rotten.

Everything I experience, I express it in written form. My poems carry a message that includes how I was able to overcome. I enjoy being able to share my gift with others especially when the message behind the words in a poem carries a sense of healing. Healing is what I have experienced. I am no longer in that place of darkness and it shows by the type of poems written in "Waterfalls." God has me in a place of forgiveness. I am at peace with my life and I no longer dwelled on material things I lost or time I lost holding on to someone in a selfish relationship. I am content with being me. I will never allow anyone to try to change me to be someone other than myself. I have been hurt so much, but now I can look back over my life and see from where God has brought me. My heart is overwhelmed with the direction my life is going. I am happy with the accomplishments I have made and the progress I have made getting up after falling so low. I am no longer holding on to the anger and bitterness I have been feeling for all these years.

I realized that in order to get past the dark areas in my life, I had to take my life in a new direction. I had to let go and turn loose. I had to dismiss and disconnect from a relationship that I had been in for far too many years. I was aging! I was getting older but what I needed was to get wiser. I realized that I had outgrown that relationship but it was not until I realized that the person I thought would eventually love me never really valued me. I had put in what seems like a lifetime with someone manipulating me into believing that "having a piece of man was better than having no man at all." It was when I said, "I want more," then just like the water flowing in a waterfall, my life began to flow. I had an appetite for love that a piece of man could not curb.

I had been starving myself of happiness. I was stuck in a relationship where I was settling. Neither happy nor content, I was letting my life drift away like debris floating down a stream of water. I knew what I wanted but what I was accepting, posed a conflict between my mind and my heart. When I allowed the things I was accepting to take preference over the things I wanted, the relationship became a battlefield. I was fighting, but only with myself. Somewhere down the line, I had lost myself and put no value on my heart. When I came to terms with the fact that I was working too hard at this thing I called love, I quit! This love was a job that paid me nothing, so I gave no notice or warning.

True love is something you should not have to put in a lot of sweat and tears. It was time to wise up. I had to set relationship goals and put a value on my time. I could no longer negotiate with my terms of endearment. I had to remove things and people from my life. Never again will I allow one person the time to tie up years and years of my life when there is no growth. I can no longer let people that add no meaning to my life hinder me. I realized that I was not going anywhere. I was blocking my own blessings trying to hold on to what God was showing me time after time meant me no good.

The poems in this section focus on the healing that has taken place in my life. They emphasize growth and display me in a place of peace and happiness. This new direction in my life has changed me for the better. I am truly a better person, friend, and companion. I stay away from negative people and dream killers. I no longer dwell on things or people that are not uplifting or beneficial in my life. A broken heart can mend and "Letting Go" was the medicine I needed, along with that amazing drug called "Forgiveness," that allowed me to be able to move forward in life.

Finding Closure

I have been very angry and very sad
I have been hurt and very mad
A dark place I struggled to get out
For years and years, I wondered about
Why I was not happy, but you appeared to be
And I wondered why no good ever came to me
So I prayed to God to show me the way
And He woke me up to see a brighter day
God removed the hate I held in my heart
He removed the chains so to heal I could start
He put me in a place of happiness and peace
Revealed when **"Finding Closure,"** I'll start to increase

Finally...Finding Closure!

I Never Stop Loving You

I never stop loving you
Some things we just cannot replace
The years I have spent with you
Are memories I will never erase

I never stop loving you
Our relationship was at a dead end
Our hearts detoured in different directions
And on each other we could no longer depend

I never stop loving you
Our time together just came to an end
Too many years was put into a relationship
One that was just too broken to mend

I never stop loving you
We somehow just grew apart
Our lives were no longer on one accord
And seems love no longer filled the heart

I never stop loving you
You are the father of my child is one reason
But my child has grown up and so have I
And everything in life has its own season

I never stop loving you…our season just ended!

Ask God to Send You a Man

When you search your heart to find love
And realize that it is still missing a beat
One that is on the same accord
With someone you cannot wait to meet

You want it to be love and not just lust
You want him to be the one God sends your way
You want him to be the one you been waiting for
You want him to be the one that's going to stay

Finding that perfect piece of puzzle
Is like finding a needle in a hay stack
Your eyes can be looking straight at it
But you can't see it for looking back

Looking back at what you once had
Reminiscing on what little joy was in your life
Forgetting about the pain you endured
And that you weren't good enough to be his wife

Your future dwells on what is present
So why would you dwell on the past
Know that God has a plan for your life
And that plan will not fail but last

You should seek God first and foremost
You should ask God to show you His plan
Stop dwelling on what could have been
And Ask God to Send You a Man

God's Chosen Rib

In life we go through certain things
We sometime find difficult to understand
If only we could just let it all go
And put our trust solely in God's hand

You'll never know what is in God's plan
Until it all unfolds before your eyes
And it will never be revealed unto you
If you continue with the what ifs and whys

It was God's plan for man and woman
To be one as husband and wife
He never said the road would be easy
Nor free from heartaches and strife

He intended for you to cry out for help
When your burdens are more than you can bear
God said, "I will never leave you nor forsake you"
And He promises to always be there

God took a rib from man and made woman
No instructions were needed to attach
And in order for that chosen rib to work
God made it to be the perfect match

God's "Will" is perfect for each one of us
And if you have a rib that starts to detach
That rib may not be in God's "Will" for you
Because God's Chosen Rib is a perfect match

I Have Waited and Waited for Someone

I have waited and waited for someone
Someone to come sweep me off my feet
Along came you at a needed time
You were someone I was destined to meet

I have waited and waited for someone
To treat me with the respect that you do
Showering me with so much affection
And being concerned about my feelings too

I have waited and waited for someone
But acceptance is how it has to be
I promise not to try to change who you are
And from you I expect the same for me

I have waited and waited for someone
Someone to be honest and true
Someone who is not afraid to commit
Someone I can give my heart to

I Have Waited and Waited for Someone…
THAT SOMEONE IS YOU!

What Matters the Most

What matters the most
Is the love that we share
The pain felt from the past
It is no longer there

My heart is rejoicing
For this love I have found
I have a peace of mind now
And I am no longer bound

What matters the most
No more shackles are on me
The chains have been removed
And the blinders too so I can see

What matters the most
I only focus on the good
My heart is open to forgiveness
Now I can love the way I should

THAT IS… WHAT MATTERS THE MOST!

Back in Love Again!

I didn't realize what was missing in my life
You opened my eyes when you came along
You showed me a different kind of love
And you put in my heart a new song

You treat me with so much respect
You are a gentlemen in every way
My heart smiles when I am with you
I could spend time with you everyday

You don't judge or look down on me
As others close to me tend to do
You don't point fingers or criticize
And your feelings for me are true

You accept me for the person I am
And for you I will do the same
The only thing about me you can change
It would have to be my name

I let go of the past that had me bound
Now this new era in my life I can begin
With someone I think is so special
Cause I realize, I'm **Back in Love Again!**

At Last! At Last! At Last!

At Last! At Last! At Last!
My love has come along
I'm dancing with a new rhythm
I'm singing to a new song
I'm with someone I can depend on
I'm with someone I can trust
To give my heart and soul to
To share love with and not lust

At Last! At Last! At Last!
I have reason to smile every day
Someone loves me for who I am
And that's something I can truly say
He's not trying to change the way I think
He's not trying to change the way I talk
He's not trying to change the way I dress
He's not trying to change the way I walk

At Last! At Last! At Last!
I'm no longer in that dark place of sadness
He tore down a wall that had me bound
And filled my heart with joy and gladness
I can't imagine my life without him
He's so different from what I had in the past
My love has finally come along
At Last! At Last! At Last!

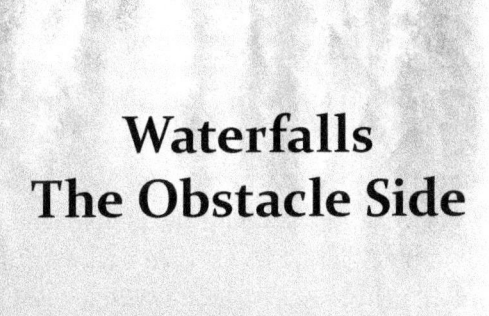

Waterfalls
The Obstacle Side

Living with a chronic illness and fighting to live another day

Waterfalls
The Obstacle Side

The obstacle side of a waterfall is what I visualize as being stage three. Here the drop is coming and just like a roller coaster, you do not know what lies beneath. In those moments of silence, you can hear the sound of the heart as it beats in a panic rhythm. The pit of the stomach is rumbling like a volcano that is about to erupt. Unimaginable thoughts wreck the beauty of a waterfall tainting their breath taking visual. I have come to that stage three in my life. I have been diagnosed with-MS (Multiple Sclerosis).

It was quite some time before I received the diagnosis that I had multiple sclerosis. My symptoms were all over the place and very hard to explain. What started out as simple falls and blurred vision soon became symptoms that were serious. What I took to be leg cramps turned out to be my joints locking up on me. It was like my body would shut down and I could not get out of bed. I ended up having a couple of pin strokes and complete numbness to the right side of my body. I had MRI's and CAT scans taken as well as other test. It was not until I experienced the awkwardness of having double vision, that the test showed there were lesions on the brain and it was multiple sclerosis. I dealt with the double vision for about two weeks. The eyeball in my right eye had shifted backwards and I could not see, walk, or maintain my balance without wearing a patch over my eye.

I kept myself isolated and confined to the house. The mobility issues were making life for me to be unbearable. It was as if my head was full of water making me nauseated and sick to the point of regurgitating every time I stood up. The temporary blindness caused fear to set in and I lose sight not only physically but I also took my eyes off God. Through my prayers, I was able to strengthen my faith. I was reminded of the scripture, "If ye have faith as a grain of mustard seed, ye shall say unto this mountain, remove hence to yonder place; and it shall remove; and nothing shall be impossible unto you (Matthew 17:20)." Standing on God's words is what helped me overcome during this difficult time. Once my eyeball shifted back into the proper position, I was able to see again.

I began to do research and found out that not only is there no cure for MS but it can cause blindness and paralyze you. Due to complications, MS can also be fatal. You can be in remission for so long and then a flare-up happens causing you to relapse. MS causes nerve damage that disrupts the communication between the brain and the body. I have to refrain from being stressed or fatigued to avoid these flare-ups. The lesions on my brain caused by MS lay dormant at this time but I must remain calm and stress free. A flare-up could cause these lesions to "wake up" and spread causing aggravation to the nerves on the brain that controls my mobility, speech, vision, and even memory.

Living with MS, has been very difficult. I have my good days and my bad days. Sometimes the bad days outweigh the good. I am in constant chronic pain and sometimes unable to walk and have normal mobility in my legs. Although in pain, I consider it a blessing because MS can paralyze you. The pain lets me know that I can feel. I am coping but it gets extremely hard sometimes and you just want the pain to go away even if it means having thoughts of suicide. I never thought I would ever think about or consider harming myself but MS can control you physically and mentally. I realize these thoughts are not normal but I do not see anything normal about MS.

MS is a storm in my life that I must weather. I find myself crying a lot. When I feel like this storm is getting the best of me, I have to steal away and have some one on one time with God. MS can be very scary because it is so unpredictable. It is almost like a cancer tearing me down in different stages. As MS affects my nervous system, I become vulnerable and hostile. Anxiety and depression rule my life sometimes making it impossible to function and interact with others. I am slowly losing sensory on the right side of my body due to MS but I am still blessed and every day is very important to me.

Although dealing with MS can be extremely difficult, things could be a lot worse. I feel blessed every day I wake up and still have the use of my limbs. I am still in my right frame of mind and I am able to walk, talk, think, and just as important to me---"WRITE." With MS, I never know what the next day will bring and it is the uncertainty that cripples me. It is the abnormal thoughts that blind me and it is the constant state of depression that paralyses me. My health has made me very dependent. I do not want to admit it but I have had to get a cane and a walker, the two things that I refuse to depend on. I look at my cane and say, "I am not giving in to this disease." I look at my walker and say, "No way, I am too young for this." When I lose my balance and fall or when I cannot get out of bed because I cannot walk, it is a reminder that I have MS and say, "I got MS but MS is not going to have me." I thank God that I am not in that stage I am dreading called the "wheelchair." I thank God that it is just a little memory loss and not a loss of me out of <u>memory</u>.

The poems in this section focus on hurdling through obstacles in your life by turning them into stepping-stones. Obstacles can be setbacks or setups. Setbacks are the ones that cause you to stumble and fall. Setups are the ones that you are able to stack on top of one another and use like a ladder to climb up and over your situation. I keep writing because I never know from one day to the next when my ability to write will cease or when my ability to think and focus will eventually diminish. MS is my stage three and just like a waterfall, I do not know what to expect when I get to the drop.

I can recall an incident that happened where my thinking was not logical and I almost overdosed. I do not know how a person feels when they overdose on drugs but all I know is it was a very scary encounter with death for me. I realized at that moment my life was in God's hands. I saw my life flash before my eyes and I was not able to do anything but silently pray to God. I could not say a word. My throat was closing up on me and I could barely breathe. This was my time alone with God to get myself together or maybe I should say my soul together to go home; hopefully to be with the Lord, cause this felt like the end. This birthed another poem for me to write titled, "When Your Life Flashes before Your Eyes."

When Your Life Flashes Before Your Eyes

When your life flashes before your eyes
What is the first thing that you would do
When time doesn't permit you to say "I'm Sorry"
And you can't cry out for anyone to help you

When you fall to your knees gasping for air
And your chest aches and your heart is pounding so fast
You don't have enough time to do nothing but pray
Because you don't know how long this feeling will last

Don't waste time trying to figure out what is happening
When God gives you time and a chance to get right
Repent so that all of your sins can and will be forgiven
Cause the Death Angel comes like a thief in the night

When your life flashes before your eyes
Take time to repent for things you have done wrong
Because for just that moment it is just you and God
And you don't know if Heaven or Hell will be your home

Multiple Sclerosis (MS)

All the aches and all the pain
Can be so very hard to bear
Hurting down to the very core
About life you suddenly do not care

You do not care if you wake up
All you want to do is sleep away
To put an end to everything
Just to not suffer another day

The pain is enough to drive you insane
Through life you stumble your way
MS is a disease so destructive
And to ease the pain to God you pray

Some people with MS lose their mind
Some people want to just end it all
Some people are not as strong as others
And do not know how on God to call

In life you feel you do not belong
MS will have depression take control of you
Agony and pain you will struggle with daily
And nothing but prayer will pull you through

Make no mistake, MS is not a joke
Complications from MS can be fatal too
But know that you can be a survivor
Because you have MS, it doesn't have to have you

This Storm I Must Weather

THIS STORM I MUST WEATHER
SOMETIMES SEEM SO HARD TO BEAR
BUT I CAN'T LET GO OF THE MASTER'S HAND
CAUSE DURING THIS STORM I KNOW HE'S THERE

I LAY AWAKE AT NIGHT WITH TEARS IN MY EYES
I PRAY FOR THE STRENGTH TO GO ON
AS I PRAY, THE TEARS THEY STOP
THEN I REALIZE ALL HOPE IS NOT GONE

THE STRENGTH I NEED COMES LIKE A GUSH OF WIND
AND I'M ABLE TO FACE ANOTHER DAY
A DAY THAT MAYBE FILLED WITH OBSTACLES
SO BEFORE I BEGIN IT, I MUST PRAY

I PRAY GOD GRANTS ME SERENITY
I PRAY MY FAITH WILL REMAIN STRONG
SO I CAN DEAL WITH THIS STORM IN MY LIFE
AND CONTINUE TO FIGHT NO MATTER HOW LONG

I PRAY GOD GRANTS ME COURAGE
COURAGE I'LL NEED TO WEATHER THROUGH
I'M FIGHTING A BATTLE I'M DETERMINED TO WIN
AND I CAN HEAR GOD SAYING, "MY CHILD, I GOT YOU"

I PRAY GOD GRANTS ME WISDOM
AND THE KNOWLEDGE I NEED TO UNDERSTAND
THAT THIS STORM I MUST WEATHER
IT TOO IS A PART OF HIS PLAN

THERE ARE THINGS IN LIFE WE CAN NOT CHANGE
LIKE GOD'S PLANS AND HIS WILL
BUT WE CAN RIDE OUT OUR STORMS
KNOWING GOD HAS THE POWER TO HEAL

THIS STORM I MUST WEATHER
IT MAY CAUSE ME TO STUMBLE
BUT KNOWING GOD IS STILL IN CHARGE
IS THE ONE THING THAT KEEPS ME HUMBLE

THIS STORM I MUST WEATHER
I CAN NOT DO IT IF I AM ALL ALONE
SO I'M THANKFUL FOR EVERYONE IN MY LIFE
BUT MOST THANKFUL FOR THE ONE ON THE THRONE

Billie Jean Mann

Fight To Live Another Day

STORMS THAT COME IN OUR LIFE ARE NEVER EASY
THE RAGING WINDS MAY CAUSE YOU TO STUMBLE AND SWAY
YOU MUST BRACE YOURSELF AND HOLD ON TIGHT
AND FIGHT TO LIVE ANOTHER DAY

WHEN THE FIGHT SEEMS TO BE AN UPHILL BATTLE
WHEN THE CLIMB TO THE TOP SEEMS SO FAR AWAY
GOD WILL GIVE YOU THE STRENGTH THAT YOU NEED
TO FIGHT TO LIVE ANOTHER DAY

WITH FAMILY AND FRIENDS RIGHT THERE BY YOUR SIDE
THE COMMUNITY TO SHOW YOU LOVE ALONG THE WAY
AND GOD WHO WILL SUPPLY YOUR EVERY NEED
AS YOU FIGHT TO LIVE ANOTHER DAY

GOD KNOWS WHEN YOU GROW WEAK AND YOU ARE TIRED
AND SOMETIMES ALL YOU NEED TO DO IS STEAL AWAY
WHAT YOU DON'T DO IS GIVE INTO YOUR SITUATION
YOU FIGHT TO LIVE ANOTHER DAY

SO WHEN YOU FIND YOURSELF ALONE IN THOUGHT
DO NOT GET DISCOURAGED OR BE DISMAY
PRAY AND ASK GOD TO HELP YOU WEATHER THIS STORM
AND YOU FIGHT TO LIVE ANOTHER DAY

Waterfalls
The Peaceful Side

Death is the final Victory!

Waterfalls
The Peaceful Side

The final stage of a waterfall puts me in touch with reality. I tried to imagine myself dropping from Niagara Falls. In that drop, death was all I could visualize. In stage four of a waterfall, I can see Death being the final victory. As we go through life, we are going to go through different stages similar to those of a waterfall. There will be particles of debris getting in the way causing life not to flow. We have to remove things out the way of our flow in order to move through life smoothly and rapidly like the water flowing in a waterfall. When things interrupt life that causes fear of the unknown, it is like going over the drop of a waterfall. When we do not survive from the drop, we have to face death, which is the final victory.

When we lose a love one, it is hard to get pass that hurt, but death can be peaceful during times of grief. All we have are the memories; therefore, we should always make lasting memories while our love ones are here with us. Give them their flowers while they can see and smell them. It is hard to say goodbye but it becomes so much easier when you know that you have picked and gave your flowers while your love one was amongst the living. Know that flowers can be something as simple as spending quality time with them, sharing a moment of joy with them or even just a visit to see how they are doing.

It is harder to accept death for those who realize that they should have done more. Your emotions are stuck between grief and grudge. Because someone held on to a grudge for years, death has now taken away his or her love one and the grudge will never be resolved. Feelings of regret set in because you realize that you let time slip away without asking the questions that needed answers. You let time slip away without forgiving your love one and now your heart is hardened. You are disappointed and feelings of being a failure cause emotional confusion. You cannot cry because you are still angry and bitter.

I have heard Death called many things. Some would say, "Death is the Gateway to Heaven." Others say, "Death is the final Victory." One thing for sure is we all will have to go through it meaning, "Death is a sure thing." It is important to forgive while you can. Resolve any issues before time steals your chance. Tomorrow is not promised nor is it a guarantee, so give your flowers today. I learned not to let the sun go down with anger in my heart. I grew up having to kiss my sisters, hug them, and tell them I love them when I call myself mad. My father did not play. You did not get angry around him and refuse to talk and show love towards one another. This taught me the true meaning of unconditional love. In my father's unique way, he wanted us to know that life is precious and you should not take it for granted. If anything happen to one of my siblings, there would be nothing to regret because we kissed, we hugged, and we said I love you enough to become a daily ritual. I thank my father for his teaching because even to this day I still do these things.

The first poem I wrote for an obituary was when my father died. I have always been able to express my feelings by writing about them. It was sad to write but as I wrote, it cleared up a lot of meaning about Death. It allowed me to find a sense of peace with Death because I saw it in a different perspective with my father. My father had been so afraid to die and tried everything possible to prolong his life. There were times when my father would cry like a helpless little child. When he realized that death was inevitable, I witnessed a transformation from him suffering to him finding peace while I was standing right there at his bedside. My father had a glow over him that looked like a halo. His skin turned golden in color and his hair silky slick like a newborn. It was as though my father had come to terms with the fact that life after death would be "Heaven."

The amazing thing I witness during my father's transformation was he spoke without any assistance to the trachea in his throat. I know now what it means when it is said, "You are an adult once but a child twice." My father curled up in a fetal position and said, "Now, I can go home."

Standing there with my mouth wide open, I knew that the home my father was speaking of was not his physical home. As shocking as it was to witness, it was the most peaceful confirmation to see that death would be our final victory. This section of poems focuses on finding peace in the mist of it all and accepting Death for what it is "our number in line."

Death

I received a call from Death today
And I usually don't answer calls I don't know
But as reluctant as I was to answer the call
I did and He said are you ready to go

Death wasted no time and grabbed my hand
And said it's your time to depart from this place
Your time on earth has come to an end
For you weathered the storms by God's grace

When Death approached me, I had no more time
I had to leave my home and love ones behind
Death is a sure thing, it's going to happen
So make preparations before you see a sign

The signs were there but I ignored them all
I thought time was a true friend of mine
I thought I had time to be more loving
I thought I had time to be more kind

Oh but I been sending up my timber, everyday
So I'll be ready when the Death angel calls my name
Making preparations to go to my new home
To receive my wings and to get my new name

Now I'll get to walk around Heaven all day
I'll get to roam the streets of gold
I'll get to sing in the Heavenly choir
And I'll get to live forever as I was told

Death is a sure thing, this you should know
So get your house in order, the Death angels roam
And when one pays you an unexpected visit
You too can say, "There's No Place Like Home"

I am not one to say Goodbye
That word seems so permanent some how
So I'll leave you with my famous departing words
And those words are "So Long for Now"

My Life Here on Earth is No More

My life here on earth has expired
Don't be sad just remember me
God has called me to come home
Home to be with Him eternally

Memories will be your keepsake
You can rest to know I am at peace
On the other side now I can rest
I can rest now that I am at peace

I jumped aboard and caught a ride
For me the sweet chariot swung low
A new life awaits for me in Heaven
My Life Here on Earth is No More

Heaven Awaits For An Angel Like Me

WISH I WAS HERE ANOTHER DAY
TO TELL YOU ALL THE THINGS I DIDN'T SAY
I WOULD SAY I LOVE YOU MORE AND MORE
AND SAY I'M MORE THANKFUL THAN BEFORE

YOU CARED FOR ME LIKE NO OTHER
I WOULD SAY TO YOU I'M GLAD TO BE YOUR MOTHER
GLAD I HAD THE CHANCE TO NURTURE YOU THROUGH LIFE
AND COMFORT YOU THROUGH YOUR HEARTACHES AND STRIFE

BE STRONG AND HOLD ON AS IF I WAS STILL WITH YOU
GOD HAS CALLED ME HOME, HE NEEDED ME TOO
FILLING HIS GARDEN WITH ANOTHER BEAUTIFUL ROSE
A ROSE LIKE ME, HE HAND PICKED AND CAREFULLY CHOSE

MEMORIES AND PICTURES OF ME YOU WILL KEEP
I'LL CONSTANTLY WHISPER IN YOUR EAR AS YOU SLEEP
I AM AND WILL FOREVER BE IN YOUR HEART
FROM YOU, I WILL NEVER EVER DEPART

ALTHOUGH I AM NOT HERE TO HOLD YOUR HAND
DO NOT QUESTION THE MASTER'S PLAN
WITH HIM, I WILL GO AND LIVE ETERNALLY
HEAVEN AWAITS FOR AN ANGEL LIKE ME

I'm Forever In Your Heart

I RECEIVED MY WINGS
NOW I MUST DEPART
DO NOT BE SAD
I'M FOREVER IN YOUR HEART

THE DEATH ANGEL CAME
I HAD NO CHOICE
AND I HAD TO GO
WHEN I HEARD GOD'S VOICE

MISS ME, I KNOW YOU WILL
THINGS WON'T BE THE SAME
THIS ANGEL HAS RECEIVED HER WINGS
AND BEEN GIVEN A NEW NAME

MY MANSION IS NOW READY
MY NEW LIFE I WILL START
CRY FOR ME NO MORE
I'M FOREVER IN YOUR HEART

REMEMBER EVERY WHERE YOU GO
FROM YOU, I WILL NEVER DEPART
IN YOUR EAR, I WILL ALWAYS WHISPER
I'M FOREVER IN YOUR HEART

A Mother's Dedication To Her Children

I was your rock when you needed me
I was always there to hold your hand
I held you up as any mother would
My leaving you now is God's plan

With wisdom and grace, I leave this place
The death angel came to carry me home
I did my best as a mother, don't you forget
Take care of one another and carry on

Times may get hard and sometimes they will
God won't put more on you than you can bear
Just when you think you are all alone
You will feel my presence in the air

The weeping endures only for a night
Shed tears if you must but not for long
Remember my strength through all of life's trials
Find strength from those memories and be strong

A mother's love was all I had to give
And that love was genuine and true
I gave and gave until I could give no more
I gave because that's what mothers do

Now dry your eyes and cry no more
It was my time to answer the call
Just remember that you are not alone
God is there should you stumble and fall

My Time Has Come To Say Goodbye

To my love ones and all my friends
My time has come to say goodbye
No longer will you hear my laughter
No longer will you hear my cry

I heard a voice that said "Come Home"
So I peacefully answered the call
A crown awaits to be put on my head
There is a crown for me and one for all

My heart was filled with kindness and gratitude
I treated everybody as I wanted them to treat me
I lived my life so my light could shine
And shine so bright that everyone could see

My earthly home I must now depart
God, I look forward to a "Closer Walk with Thee"
There is a mansion in the sky with many rooms
One of those rooms have been assigned to me

Weeping endures only just for a night
Just as sure as we live, we will die
Wipe your eyes and for me cry no more
My time has come to say goodbye

This Road I Will Travel No More

I HAVE TRAVELLED THIS ROAD MANY MANY TIMES
AND NEVER NOTICED IT HAD A DEAD END BEFORE
BUT I HAVE NOTICED THE BEAUTY SLOWLY FADING AWAY
AND THE GRASS ALONG THE SIDES WASN'T GREEN ANYMORE

AND I DIDN'T RECALL THIS ROAD BEING SO DARK
THE ONLY LIGHT I SAW WAS STRAIGHT AHEAD
I TRIED TO TURN BACK BUT NOTHING WAS THERE
SO I HAD NO CHOICE BUT TO FOLLOW THE LIGHT INSTEAD

THEN I REALIZED MY LIFE WAS COMING TO AN END
AND DEATH, I WAS FACING IT ALL ALONE
IT'S TRUE, WE DON'T KNOW THE DAY NOR HOUR
AND THE LIGHT WAS AN ANGEL GUIDING ME HOME

DARKNESS WAS BEHIND ME ALL THE WAY THERE
AT MY DESTINATION, I ENTERED THE DOOR
I TURNED AND LOOKED, AGAIN THERE WAS NOTHING
NOT EVEN THIS ROAD I WILL TRAVEL NO MORE

Time Ran Out For Me

DON'T WORRY ABOUT TOMORROW
IT WILL HAVE ENOUGH TROUBLES OF ITS OWN
TIME RAN OUT FOR ME
I ANSWERED TO THE ONE ON THE THRONE

MY JOURNEY HAS COME TO AN END
MY BATTLES HAVE ALL BEEN WON
MY BURDENS, I HAVE NO MORE
MY RACE, I CAN NO LONGER RUN

TIME RAN OUT FOR ME
I DID NOT GIVE UP WITHOUT A FIGHT
THE FIGHT JUST GOT TOO HARD
BUT I FOUGHT WITH ALL MY MIGHT

I GREW WEAK AND I WAS TIRED
I SAW A LIGHT AND I SHED A TEAR
GOD WAS CALLING ME TO COME HOME
I KNEW THE DEATH ANGEL HAD TO BE NEAR

I WOULD LOVE TO LIVE TO DIE ANOTHER DAY
BUT WE DON'T KNOW THE DAY NOR HOUR
TIME RAN OUT FOR ME
AND TODAY I BECAME GOD'S FLOWER

I'll See You Come through the Pearly Gates Too

I was not put here to stay forever
For everything happens for a reason
My time on earth has come to an end
This means it is the end of my season

My walk on earth has been pleasant
But I want to walk the streets of gold
Sing and do my Heavenly dance
And live forever like I was told

I want to claim my room in the mansion
I want to walk around Heaven all day
Sing praises in the Heavenly choir
And thank Jesus for the price He had to pay

I want to hear God say, "Well Done"
I want to see my Master's face
I want to forever be in His presence
To hear Him say, "You ran a good race"

Dry your eyes and shed no more tears
To mourn for me you must not do
Prepare your life for when this day comes
"I'll see you come through the pearly gates too"

Life is so uncertain living with MS. This poem, "I'll See You Come Through the Pearly Gates Too," was written for when my number in line is called and I achieve my final victory.

Waterfalls
Black Lives Matter

Unjustifiable deaths can cause tears worldwide to flow like water in a waterfall.

Waterfalls
Black Lives Matter

I added this section to "Waterfalls," because racism is still flowing very rapidly, like the water flows in a waterfall. It is so true that "the more things change, the more they stay the same." This world is so full of hatred. Those in authority are constantly teaching racism. They are teaching racism by displaying their actions to be the right way to treat people. Growing up in a small town, I have witnessed racism in the school system. The teachers were bias when it came to allowing a black person to be equal to a white person. As a black person, I had to work harder for my grades in school. It did not matter how smart you were, you were not going to get the recognition you deserved. I had teachers that actually taught by their actions that whites were better. I even walked up on a teacher in the hallway scolding one of my classmates to believe he was more deserving of the reward of salutatorian, a position we both deserved. I was told there could not be two salutatorians and that I should be honored as a top student by doing the benediction. I saw this as a "Rosa Parks" moment and refused.

Vital information you needed was deliberately withhold until the last minute and you had no chance of getting any scholarships you were entitled. I learned from my experiences and I try to teach black students not to wait on anyone to give them information. They need to demand it. Do not let a bias teacher determine your destiny. I hope the school systems today have changed.

 On jobs, you will experience racism as well. Black people are treated less than equal. They receive less pay and are given jobs those in authority feel they are best suited for instead of jobs they are equally qualified for. We as black people have to prove ourselves to be worthy of anything we receive. Have you ever had to train a white person for a job promotion you should have been next in line for? It is a tough pill to swallow. Things like this show there is no real progress in the mindset of some white people in charge. Again, I am talking about things I have experienced.

My advice to anyone is to know your worth. There is no one, white or black, that is better than you are. We may not be treated equally but we were all created equally. Do not settle for less than your worth. Do not be put in a box and allow someone to lock you in. Do not let racism control your destiny. The key to your success is in your hands.

Racism in any form is deadly. It can kill dreams and take away lives. The hate that someone holds in his or her heart can cause a lot of chaos. I am remembering several events that occurred that caused a lot of chaos all over the world. These events made history by exposing racism at an all time high. Cops were killing black men and black women with no remorse. Several of these killings have been deemed unjustifiable. A black woman was shot and killed by police officers using a "No Knock" entry tactic to conduct a search. A young black man minding his own business, out for a daily jog was stalked, gunned down and killed while being filmed by a white racist civilian. There were many other hate crimes towards blacks, all causing chaos, but one in particular shook the whole world and weighed heavily on my heart.

The death of one young man caused protesters to assemble all around the United States, marching and yelling "Black Lives Matter" in all fifty states at the same time. Seeing the actions being carried out on Mr. George Floyd on national television, had me shedding tears and lead to the birth of a poem highlighting the police brutality that he suffered for over nine minutes. Worldwide tears flowed like water flowing down a waterfall. Because of his death, the world marched in multitudes for a change to occur. The country being in the middle of a global pandemic now had to worry about senseless killings of blacks by those who are supposed to "Serve and Protect" not "Serve to Kill." The poem "I Can't Breathe" was written in loving memory of this young man, Mr. George Floyd.

I Can't Breathe

"I CAN'T BREATHE," "I CAN'T BREATHE"
THE LAST WORDS YOU WILL REMEMBER ME SAYING
YOUR KNEE ON MY NECK
WHILE ON THE ASPHALT I WAS LAYING

BEGGING FOR YOU TO HAVE A HEART
BEGGING FOR SOME FORM OF EMPATHY
BUT BECAUSE OF YOUR ABUSE OF AUTHORITY
THE WORLD IS NOW EXPRESSING THEIR DEEPEST SYMPATHY

YOUR FACE IS NO LONGER COVERED WITH CLOTH
YOU NOW HIDE BEHIND A BADGE AND UNIFORM
I WAS JUST ANOTHER BLACK MAN
ONE WHO DONE OR MEANT YOU NO HARM

YOU DIDN'T SET FIRE AND BURN A CROSS
YOU DIDN'T BEAT ME AND HANG ME FROM A TREE
BUT YOU SHOWED YOUR HATRED FOR BLACKS
WHEN YOU KNEELED ON MY NECK UNTIL YOU KILLED ME

GASPING FOR AIR I CRIED, "I CAN'T BREATHE"
OTHER MEMBERS OF YOUR KLAN JUST STOOD AROUND
WATCHING A HOPELESS BLACK MAN CRY OUT FOR HIS MOMMA
YOUR HANDS IN YOUR POCKETS AND I'M PINNED TO THE GROUND

BUT MY DEATH WILL NOT BE IN VAIN
AND MY PURPOSE WILL SOON BE REVEALED
ONE BY ONE THE MASK WILL COME OFF
AND FROM RACISM THIS LAND WILL BE HEALED

GOD MADE US ALL IN HIS IMAGE
AND EVERYONE ON EARTH HAS A PURPOSE TO FULFILL
BUT RACISM CAUSES SOME TO DISOBEY GOD
BY IGNORING HIS COMMANDMENT, "THY SHALL NOT KILL"

LIKE MARTIN LUTHER KING JR, I WILL CHANGE THE WORLD
I DIED AT THE HANDS OF THOSE WHOSE HEARTS WERE FULL OF HATE
BUT RACISM IS SOMETHING THAT ONE HAS TO BE TAUGHT
BECAUSE WE WERE ALL BORN INTO THIS WORLD WITH A CLEAN SLATE

THE LAST WORDS I SPOKE WILL BRING ABOUT A CHANGE
MANY WILL KNOW ME AND REMEMBER MY NAME
FOR UNTIL THERE IS JUSTICE, THERE IS NO PEACE
AND BECAUSE OF MY DEATH, THE WORLD WILL NEVER BE THE SAME

"PLEASE, I CAN'T BREATHE…MOMMA"

Closing Remarks

There is so much that I love about waterfalls. I love the way they look. I love the way they sound. I love the mood they bring to the atmosphere. I have a ceramic waterfall that I turn on and just being in the room listening to the soothing sound of the water hitting the rocks at the bottom puts me in touch with reality. This book, "Waterfalls," was written based on my life in comparison to the beauty and different stages of a waterfall. Before I could even begin to write, "Waterfalls," I had to ask myself some questions in regards to my life. I wanted to know what I had to do to get pass the hurt that has caused me to continuously stumble through life. There was a hole in my heart that would not allow love to enter. I needed to know what was in my pathway that would not allow me to move forward and flow like the water that flows in a waterfall.

In this book, "Waterfalls," I focused on the brighter side, the obstacle side, and the peaceful side of waterfalls. I have an incurable disease that affects me mentally and physically. This disease causes me to struggle to keep my sanity. I had to create a safe haven where I could go to collect my thoughts. I saw that my life had been in different stages just like those I visualized in a waterfall. Because I was obedient to the Word of God, I had to forgive those who hurt me. It was not easy but I wanted to live, laugh, and love again.

When writing these poems, I saw that I was in a much brighter place in my life and found myself more at peace and much happier. Just like the characteristics that I see in a waterfall, these poems are peaceful, calming and soothing. The hurt I had experienced was no longer an issue and show through the poetry in "Waterfalls." This shows that healing has occurred in my life. The hole in my heart has been filled with love that has value. That love is the love I have for myself. I have let go of the pain, hurt, and disappointments from others that I allowed to control me. My life is flowing now that I am no longer bitter or resentful. I will never let anyone cloud my judgment, waste valuable time in my life, nor occupy space in my heart that I have allotted for real love. If someone is not there to contribute to the growth and prosperity that I deserve, I need them to keep it moving so my "BOAZ" can see me gleaming out in the field.

I have a battle to fight and it is not with somebody who can up and leave me. The battle I have to fight is with a sickness that will never leave me. Although I struggle with MS and live my life daily in agony and pain, waterfalls remind me of God's grace and mercy and that they both endure forever. I do not look at MS as an obstacle, but as a storm. Growing up, I learned that whenever there is a storm, you are to sit still, remain quiet and let God handle His business. When I sit and listen to the sound that comes from a waterfall, I am able to visualize myself in a secluded place that is full of palm trees and colorful flowers. The soothing sound helps me meditate and forget about the pain. It also helps me stay focused on living. Every day is a struggle, but every day is a blessing. Despite the pain, depression and mental thoughts of giving up, being in that secluded place I am able to connect with God spiritually. I am able to thank Him for yet another day.

If you think you know my pain, YOU DON'T! I carry my pain with a smile on my face. Whatever thoughts I have that makes dying seems to be a better choice, I am so glad to know that I can call on the name of Jesus. Those thoughts are as debris trapped on a limb in a waterfall, but the name JESUS, is like a mighty gush of wind that blows those thoughts right out of my mind. JESUS! JESUS! JESUS! There is definitely something about that name.

www.ingramcontent.com/pod-product-compliance
Lightning Source LLC
Chambersburg PA
CBHW032218040426
42449CB00005B/650